Contents

Acknowledgements
Thanks to David Oxley for compiling the text.
The publishers would like to thank Puma, Umbro and Medisport for their photographic contributions to this book.

Photographs on the outside and inside covers courtesy of Allsport UK Ltd.
Photographs on pages 1, 6, 29, 30, 31, 34, 38, 40 and 43 courtesy of Sporting Pictures (UK) Ltd.
Illustrations by Ron Dixon of Taurus Graphics.

Note Throughout the book players and officials are referred to individually as 'he'. This should, of course, be taken to mean 'he or she' where appropriate. All measurements are in metric units; an imperial conversion table is given on page 47.

Introduction

The game of rugby league football was born directly out of one of the greatest sporting rows of all time. Throughout the early 1890s, many rugby union clubs in the north of England were continually at loggerheads with the game's governing body, the London-based Rugby Football Union, over allegations that in order to accommodate the characteristically competitive nature of northern rugby they were offering inducements for players to change clubs, and that some clubs were actually paying players to play for them. Such allegations were seldom proven, but an increasing number of northern clubs openly wished to make 'broken time' payments, i.e. to compensate their players for bona fide loss of wages incurred as a result of travelling to play in away matches.

The principle of broken time payments was strenuously opposed by the Rugby Football Union, and in April 1893 at a tempestuous special general meeting of the governing body held in London, a proposal by northern clubs that broken time payments should be permitted was defeated.

A split was inevitable. In August 1895, 21 clubs attending an historic meeting in Huddersfield voted to break away from the Rugby Football Union and form a new separate body called the 'Northern Rugby Football Union'.

For the first two seasons or so the new body played to the old rugby union rules, but the need to make the game more exciting to attract the spectators on whom the clubs depended for their financial support saw the introduction of a number of important changes in the rules, eventually producing the distinctive characteristics of the 13-a-side code. The last vestige of a connection with the Rugby Union disappeared in 1922 when the Northern Union changed its name to the 'Rugby Football League'.

Though the sceptics gave the new break-away code little chance of survival, rugby league is now firmly established as one of the world's major spectator and participant sports.

Whereas professional rugby league is still largely confined to the north of England, some 1200 clubs play the game at amateur level on a nationwide basis. Many of these run junior sections beginning with the six to eight year age group. Rugby league is particularly strong in the universities, not only in England but also in Wales, Scotland and Ireland, and the game has suffered far less than most at schools level, where there is still plenty of activity in the wide-ranging competitions run by the English Schools Rugby League. The Civil Service and various police forces are other well-established areas of activity.

Further afield, rugby league football is played extensively in Australia, New Zealand, France, Papua New Guinea, and also in Fiji, Western Samoa, Tonga, the Cook Islands, South Africa and in some of the new countries established following the break-up of the former Soviet Union.

The game

The game of rugby league is played by two teams, each with 13 players. The object of the game is to score tries and kick goals. A try is scored by a player grounding the ball in his opponents' in-goal, and a goal is scored by kicking the ball between the opponents' goal posts and above the cross-bar. A try counts four points. A conversion or a penalty goal counts two points. A dropped goal counts one point. The team gaining the highest number of points wins the match.

The field

Fig. 1 on page 4 illustrates the markings and dimensions of the playing area. The area should be as near as is practical to the maximum dimensions, although smaller pitches are permissible for youngsters' games. Minimum dimensions are stipulated in the rules governing the particular league or competition in which the game is being played. Marking lines should be clearly defined, uniform in width (not more than 100 mm) and made with whiting or chalk. Ruts should not be cut in the turf.

Goal posts

On each goal line and equidistant from the touch lines are two upright posts joined by a cross-bar, called goal posts. Dimensions are shown in fig. 2 on page 4. For the purpose of judging a kick at goal, the upright posts are considered to extend indefinitely upwards, and thus the taller the posts the easier the task of the adjudicating official.

The cross-bar must not extend beyond the goal posts.

It is a common practice for clubs to wrap rubber pads around the bases of the posts as protection for the players.

Flag posts

Posts, which should bear flags, are placed at the corners of the goal line

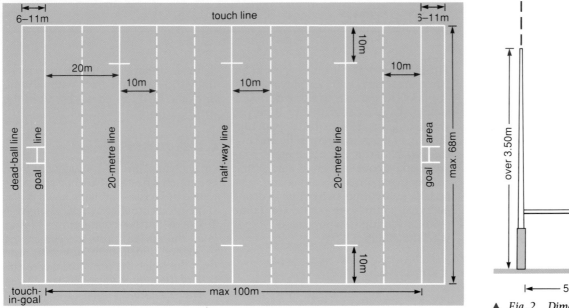

▲ *Fig. 1   The field of play*

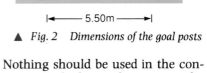

▲ *Fig. 2   Dimensions of the goal posts*

and the touch line. They must be made of non-rigid material and be not less than 1.2 m high.

The ball

The game is played with an oval ball, the outer casing of leather or other approved material enclosing an air-inflated bladder. The dimensions and weight are as shown in fig. 3.

Nothing should be used in the construction which might injure the players.

If the ball becomes deflated during play, the referee should blow his whistle and immediately stop the game.

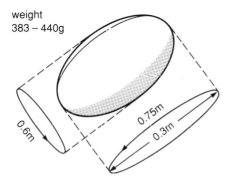

weight
383 – 440g

0.6m
0.75m
0.3m

▲ *Fig. 3   Dimensions of the ball*

The players

There are 13 players on either side at the start of the game. Any two players, irrespective of whether they are injured, may be replaced by substitutes at any time provided that the replacements are sanctioned by the referee and that the names of the two substitutes are made known to the referee before the game commences. In England a team may make a maximum of four changes for any reason and at any time during the game.

No. 7, the 'scrum-half', is the player who places the ball in the scrum.

No. 9, the 'hooker', is the player who attempts to 'rake' the ball from the scrum with his foot.

Players' equipment

The players of one side all wear the same coloured jerseys and shorts. These are usually numbered, each number indicating the position of the wearer. If the referee thinks that the similarity between the colours of the jersey of two opposing sides is likely to cause confusion, he may instruct the away side to use jerseys of a different colour.

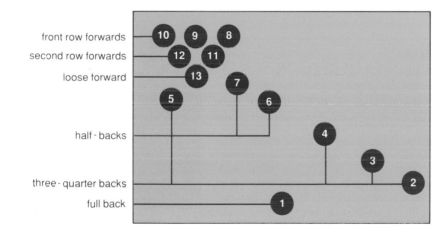

front row forwards
second row forwards
loose forward
half-backs
three-quarter backs
full back

◀ *Fig. 4   Players' positions: 1 – full back; 2 – right wing three-quarter; 3 – right centre three-quarter; 4 – left centre three-quarter; 5 – left wing three-quarter; 6 – stand-off half-back or outside half; 7 – scrum-half or inside half; 8 front row prop forward; 9 – hooker; 10 – front row prop forward; 11 – second row forward; 12 – second row forward; 13 – loose forward*

5

Players should be smart in appearance. A smart team is not necessarily a good team, but a good team is invariably of smart appearance.

Some players, particularly forwards, choose to wear a shoulder harness for protection. Head protectors, or 'scrum caps', are also sometimes worn. It is strongly recommended that a gum shield is worn to act as a shock absorber for the mouth. The gum shield should be individually tailored to a player's dental profile by an orthodontist. All such protective equipment should be of a design approved by the governing body's medical panel.

Boots

A player should take great care of his boots. Long studs are more useful on soft ground than short studs. Studs on boots must be no less than 8 mm in diameter at the apex and, if made of metal, must have rounded edges. It is the duty of the referee to order a player to remove any part of his equipment which is likely to cause injury to other players, for example projecting nails on boots, or rings on fingers.

▲ *Shirt and shorts*

▲ *Some players choose to wear a 'scrum cap'*

▲ *It is strongly recommended that a gum shield is worn*

▲ *Boots*

The officials

All matches are controlled by an appointed referee and two touch judges under the control of the referee.

The referee

The referee is mainly responsible for the control of the game. He enforces the laws of the game during play, is the sole time-keeper, unless time-keepers are appointed, and keeps a record of the scores (time-keepers were made compulsory in the English professional game with effect from the 1972/73 season). To do this he carries a whistle (and a spare), which he blows when he wishes to stop the play, a notebook and pencils. He should also have a coin with which the opposing captains can toss for choice of ends.

His dress should be of a colour easily distinguishable from the colours of the players' jerseys.

At his discretion the referee may allow extra time for delays and time wasted, and may also suspend a game if he thinks it necessary. He may dismiss from the field of play any player who persistently and wilfully breaks the laws or who is guilty of foul play or misconduct. If, in the referee's judgement, a player is guilty of misconduct of a less serious nature, the referee may impose a temporary dismissal under which the guilty player must leave the field of play for 10 minutes (the 'sin bin'). If a player is bleeding profusely the referee must order him to leave the field for treatment. During his absence a substitute may take his place and if the injured player returns to take his place within 15 minutes, then that substitution does not count towards the maximum number of changes (four) allowed under the substitution rules currently operating in England. Reports of all untoward incidents should be forwarded by the referee to the organisation under the jurisdiction of which the game is being played.

Having given a decision the referee cannot alter it unless a new decision on an earlier incident is required, for example a touch judge reports that the ball has been in touch. In certain cases the non-offending side may be penalised should the referee stop the game for an infringement, thus losing the advantage they may have and perhaps

the opportunity to score. In such a case the referee should allow play to continue and the non-offending team to maintain its advantage.

The success of the game depends largely on the referee, who should keep up with the play, be neutral at all times in his decisions, and limit stoppages to a minimum. The players are under the control of the referee from the time they enter the playing area until the time they leave it.

In all professional games a fourth official, the reserve referee, is always on hand to take over from the original referee should he be incapacitated during the game, and to administer sin-bin and blood-bin situations.

In Australia an in-goal judge operates at either end of the field to assist the referee in adjudicating directly on situations which occur in the in-goal area.

◀ *The officials: the referee flanked by his touch judges*

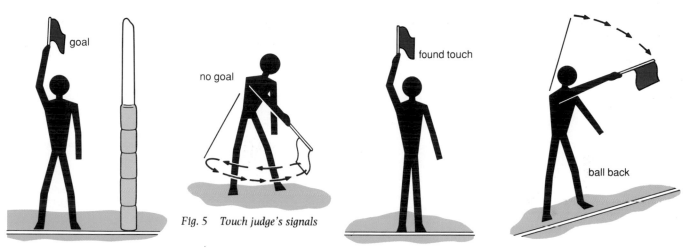

Fig. 5   Touch judge's signals

The touch judge

The touch judge decides where the ball goes into touch. He is also delegated by the referee to adjudicate kicks at goal, in which case if the kick is successful he indicates that a goal has been scored by raising his flag above his head. He signals 'no goal' by waving his flag across the front of his body below his waist. To indicate that a player has 'found touch' he runs immediately to the point where the ball enters touch and stands there with flag upraised until the game restarts. It is restarted by forming a scrum on the 10-metre line opposite where he stands (*see* page 11) except in the case of a penalty kick to touch (*see* page 12). If he wishes to indicate 'ball back', i.e. the ball is kicked forwards and enters touch on the full, he waves his flag above his head, accentuating the backward movement. In this case the game is restarted by forming a scrum where the ball was kicked (*see* page 12).

The touch judge may also call the referee's attention to any foul play which escaped the latter's notice.

When a penalty kick is being taken, the nearer touch judge takes up a position near the touch line 10 m beyond the mark to act as a marker for the team which is required to retire. He will wave his flag horizontally in front of him if any player fails to retire the required 10 m.

9

Duration of the game

In senior competitions the game invariably lasts 80 minutes and is divided into two equal halves, between which there is a 5 minutes' interval. At half-time the teams change ends.

The referee blows his whistle to indicate half-time or full-time. He should not blow for half-time or full-time until the ball is out of play, or a player in possession is being tackled.

If a penalty kick has been awarded, the referee must allow it to be taken before blowing for half-time or full-time. Time should be extended to allow for the second kick to be taken in the event of the penalty kick being kicked into touch.

Choice of ends

Before the game starts the home captain tosses a coin in the presence of the referee, giving the visiting captain the call. The winner of the toss will choose which goal his team will defend, and the loser will take the kick-off.

After the interval the kick-off is taken by the team which did not kick off to start the game.

Rules of play

The kick-off

After the choice of ends the teams line up in their respective halves of the field and the game is commenced by a place kick taken by any player of the side awarded the kick-off. The ball is placed at the centre of the half-way line and must be kicked forwards beyond the opponents' 10-metre mark. All players of the kicker's side must remain behind the half-way line until after the ball has been kicked forwards. The game is

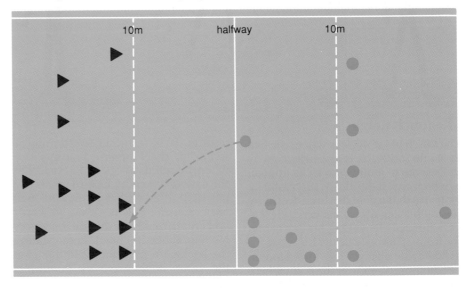

▲ *Fig. 6   The kick-off*

recommenced in a similar manner after points have been scored and at the start of the second half of the game.

When the ball is kicked off, the kicker must kick the ball 10 m or more in a forward direction, and no one on his side should touch the ball before it has travelled 10 m forwards. Any infringement of this rule will result in a penalty kick being awarded against the kicker's side at the centre spot.

The opposing team must not advance beyond the 10-metre mark and prevent the ball from travelling 10 m forwards, otherwise a penalty kick at the centre spot will be awarded against them.

After the kick-off the ball may be kicked or picked up by any player. A player may 'find touch' from the kick-off, provided that the ball travels at least 10 m forwards and bounces in the field of play before crossing the touch line. If he kicks directly over the touch line, however, a penalty is awarded against him. This also applies should the ball be kicked dead on the full. In both cases a penalty kick at the centre spot is awarded against the offending team.

Ball in and out of play

The ball is out of play when it goes into touch, is made 'dead', or when the referee stops the game.

Touch

The ball is in touch when:

● it touches the ground *on* or *over* the touch line (the touch line itself being out of play)
● although in the field of play, it is touched by a player who is himself in touch
● a player carrying it steps on or touches the touch line or the ground outside the touch line.

In play

The ball is *not* in touch when:

● it crosses the touch line in the air and swerves or is blown back into the field of play before bouncing
● a player standing inside the field of play reaches over the touch line and catches the ball before it touches the ground.

Note A player is not allowed to throw the ball forwards deliberately, and should he do so a penalty is awarded against him, whether or not the ball subsequently goes into touch.

When the ball goes into touch in the normal course of play or is carried over the touch line by a player, a scrum is formed opposite the point where the ball crossed or touched the line and 10 m inside the field of play.

Finding touch

A player can gain ground by 'finding touch', i.e. by kicking the ball forwards so that it first bounces in the field of play before entering touch. In this case a scrum is formed opposite the point where the ball crossed the touch line, 10 m inside the field. At the scrum, the non-kicking side has the advantage of the loose head and feeding the ball into the scrummage.

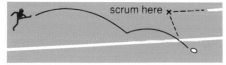

▲ *Fig. 7   Finding touch*

11

Ball back

A player cannot gain ground by kicking the ball forwards so that it enters touch without first bouncing in the field of play except from a penalty kick.

Kicking the ball into touch on the 'full' is referred to colloquially as 'ball back' – to signify that no ground has been gained, and that the scrum is formed where the ball was kicked. This does not apply to a place kick from the centre. In this case a penalty is awarded against the kicker.

It is important to note that a player can gain ground from a penalty kick by kicking the ball into touch on the full, when in this case the kicker's side is allowed to regain possession of the ball by taking a second kick 10 m in from touch opposite the point of entry into touch.

If a player kicks the ball from his own in-goal and it goes into touch on the full (see A1, fig. 9), the game is restarted with a drop-out from between the posts (see A2, fig. 9). It is permissible, however, for a player to find touch with a kick from his own in-goal, the ball in that case bouncing in the field of play before going into touch (see B, fig. 9).

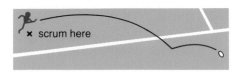

▲ *Fig. 8   Ball back*

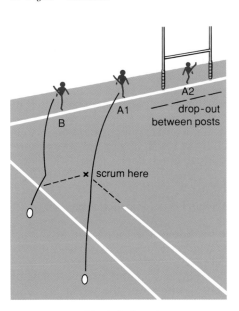

▲ *Fig. 9   Ball back: kicking from own in-goal*

Dead ball

If the ball is kicked or carried over the dead-ball line or touched down by a defender or kicked into touch on the full by a defender, the game is restarted by the defending side drop kicking from between the goal posts.

If the ball is kicked over the touch-in-goal line or dead-ball line by an attacking player or an attacking player infringes in the opponents' in-goal, the game is restarted by the defending side placing the ball from the centre of the 20-metre line and kicking it forwards. A player may tap the ball forwards and regain it himself providing the ball has crossed the 20-metre line. If, following a kick-off, the ball bounces in the field of play and is subsequently touched by or touches a defending player, or is not touched by a defending player, before it passes over the dead-ball line or into touch-in-goal, the game is restarted with a drop-out by a defending player from the centre of his goal line.

Touch down

In the case of a drop-out, the side not kicking the ball must retire 10 m from the appropriate line, i.e. the goal line or the 20-metre line.

If the drop kicker kicks out of the field of play on the full, a penalty is awarded against him – between the posts and 10 m from the goal line in the case of a drop-out from between the posts, and on the centre of the 20-metre line in the case of a drop-out from the 20-metre line.

Scoring – a try

● A try is scored by an attacking player placing the ball on the ground in his opponents' in-goal area, providing the player is not himself in touch, in touch-in-goal, or over the dead-ball line. The try is awarded at the spot where the player grounds the ball.
● A try is also awarded if an attacking player carrying the ball touches an official or spectator in his opponents' in-goal, the try being awarded at the point where the player touched the official or spectator.
● The referee may also award a try to a player if, in his opinion, the player would have scored but for unfair play by the defending team. In this case the try is awarded between the posts, irrespective of where the offence took place.
● A try is awarded if a tackled player's momentum carries him into the opponents' in-goal, where he grounds the ball, even if the ball has first touched the ground in the field of play, but provided that when the ball crosses the goal line the player is not in touch or touch-in-goal, or on or over the dead-ball line. This is commonly referred to as a 'sliding try'.

Note The goal line is itself within the in-goal area, so that a player may score by placing the ball on the goal line.

Scoring – a goal

A goal is scored by kicking the ball from the field of play over the opponents' cross-bar, except from a kick-off, drop-out, punt or fly-kick. A fly-kick is a kick at a loose ball, i.e. a ball which is not held by any player.

Thus a goal may be scored by:

● improving a try
● a drop kick during play
● a penalty kick.

A goal is allowed if:

● the ball passes over the cross-bar and is blown back by the wind
● the ball hits the cross-bar or goal posts and rebounds over the cross-bar.

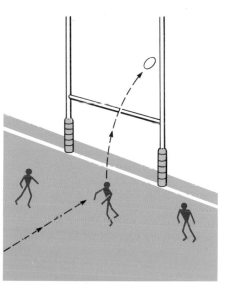

▲ *Fig. 10   No goal if the ball first touches another player before passing over the cross-bar*

13

It is not a goal if the ball first bounces on the ground or touches another player before passing over the cross-bar (*see* fig. 10 on page 13).

Improving a try

A team scoring a try is awarded a kick at goal to attempt to 'improve' the try. Thus six points are scored (four for the try and two for the goal).

The kick at goal is taken from any point within the field of play opposite the spot where the try was awarded, as shown in fig. 11.

The kick is a 'place kick', that is the ball is kicked from the ground.

Players of the defending side must stand behind their own goal line or outside the field of play, and players of the attacking side must remain behind the kicker until the kick has been taken.

After the kick at goal the defending team restarts the game with a place kick from the centre of the half-way line, irrespective of whether the kick is successful or not.

If a player fouls an opponent who is touching down for a try, a penalty kick shall be taken from in front of the posts

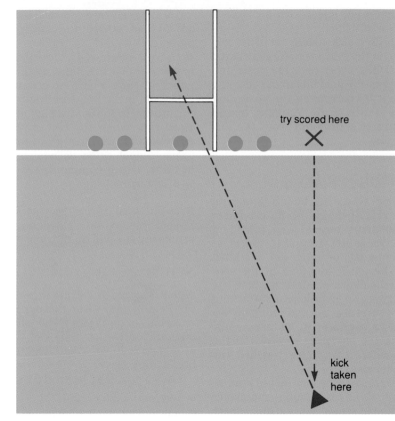

try scored here

kick taken here

▲　*Fig. 11　Improving a try*

14

after the attempt to convert the try has been made. This is called the 'eight point try' because eight points could result from the incident (four for the try, two for the conversion and two for the penalty). After the penalty kick has been taken, play is restarted from the half-way line in the normal manner after a score.

Goal from drop kick

A player may score a goal during play by dropping the ball and kicking it on the rebound so that it goes over the cross-bar. This is known as a 'drop goal' and counts one point.

Goal from penalty kick

A penalty kick may be awarded to the non-offending side for certain infringements. These are dealt with later on pages 20–7. If the non-offending team elects to attempt to kick a goal, the kick is taken from any point on or behind the place where the offence occurred and the same distance from the touch line.

The kicker may place kick or drop kick the ball.

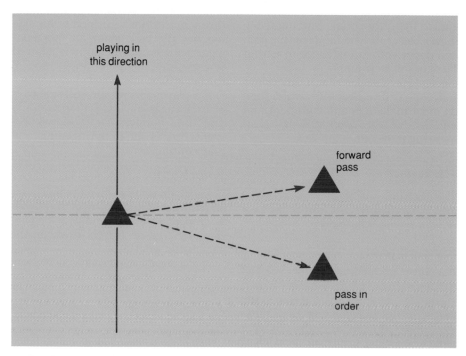

▲ *Fig. 12   Forward pass (see page 16)*

Players of the offending side must retire 10 m from the 'mark'. The mark is the term given to the spot where the penalty was awarded. Players of the non-offending side must remain behind the ball until it is kicked.

When a player intends to kick at goal from a penalty award and moves back from the mark in order to improve his angle, then the mark automatically moves back to where he places the ball, and opponents can advance to within 10 m of this new mark.

If a player signifies that he intends to kick at goal from a penalty award, then he must make a genuine attempt and not deceive the opposition by commencing play with a tap kick.

Passing

The ball may be thrown or knocked from one player to another in any direction except forwards.

Forward pass

If a player accidentally throws the ball in a forward direction to one of his own team, the referee awards a scrum at the place the infringement occurs. However, if in the opinion of the referee a player in giving a forward pass must have been well aware that the catcher was in front of him, then the referee should rule that the ball has been deliberately thrown forwards and award a penalty to the opponents.

Note If a player makes a forward

throw but before he or one of his side touches the ball again an opponent gains possession, the game is allowed to continue. This is an application of the advantage law.

If a player throws the ball sideways or backwards and it falls to the ground and then bounces, or is blown forwards, this is not an infringement and play continues.

Knock-on

A knock-on occurs when the ball, after touching the hand or arm of the player, is dropped to the ground in a forward direction (i.e. it travels towards the opponents' goal line).

If a player accidentally knocks on, i.e. knocks the ball forwards and catches it again before it touches the ground, play is allowed to proceed. If he knocks on and the ball falls to the ground and he or any of his side gains an immediate advantage, for example his side regains possession, then play is stopped and a scrum is formed. If the opposing side gains the advantage, play is allowed to continue.

Should a player charge down an opponent's kick and the ball rebound

off his hand or arm, this does not constitute a knock-on and play is allowed to continue.

Tackling

A player holding the ball may be tackled by an opponent. This means that he may be grasped round the body or the legs in order to bring him to the ground with the ball in his possession or to stop his progress and prevent him from passing or kicking the ball.

It is an offence for a tackler to make contact of any sort with the head of an opponent. The degree of the penalty incurred for such an offence will depend on the referee's judgement of the seriousness of the offence. For instance, the referee will award a straightforward penalty to the non-offending side if he judges that the offence was of a less serious nature, or if he feels that the tackled player ducked into the tackle, or that the player making the tackle was acting on reflex without any malicious intent. For more serious offences, however, the referee must dismiss the offending player from the field of play either temporarily for

10 minutes (to the 'sin bin'), or for the remainder of the game if he judges that the tackler made a deliberate and vicious attack to the head of his opponent.

If a player *accidentally* loses possession of the ball after he has been tackled, a scrum shall be formed on the spot. If he *deliberately* loses possession of the ball after being tackled a penalty shall be awarded against him.

If a tackle is broken before the player in possession is grounded he may play on.

It is illegal for an opponent to 'steal' the ball from the player who is being tackled.

If a player is fairly held so that he cannot pass or kick the ball, although he has not been grounded, the referee may instruct him to 'play the ball'.

If a number of players go down together and the referee is undecided which player is in possession, he should order a scrum to be formed. A player shall not deliberately and unnecessarily allow himself to be tackled by voluntarily falling to the ground with the ball in his possession or by dropping on to the ball and remaining on it when he has time to regain his feet and continue play.

It is important to note that a tackle is considered to have taken place at the point where the tackled player's forward momentum ends. For example, a player running at full speed and tackled from behind may slide along the ground with the ball in his hands for some distance. If in such a case a tackled player crosses his opponents' goal line before coming to a stop, a try should be awarded.

Handing off

A player may elude a tackle by 'handing off' his opponent. This means he may push him off with the open palm of his hand. He must not strike or punch. A player tackled and held must 'play the ball' (*see* below).

Playing the ball

A team in possession shall be allowed five successive play-the-balls, the play-the-ball being a method of bringing the ball into play after a tackle. If a team is tackled a sixth successive time, the ball in the meantime not having been touched by an opponent, then possession of the ball is surrendered to the opponents.

When play is restarted with a play-the-ball, it is done in the following manner.

The tackler must release his opponent without delay and the player in possession must play the ball as quickly as possible. He regains his feet, faces his opponents' goal line, and drops or places the ball in front of him, after which the ball can be played in any direction by any player.

One opponent, not necessarily the tackler, may stand opposite the player playing the ball. He may stand as close as he likes provided that he does not interfere with the movements of the player in possession.

A player playing the ball more often than not heels the ball to a colleague standing behind him. This colleague is known as an 'acting half-back', and he may stand as close to the player playing the ball as he wishes provided he is directly behind.

Each side is allowed an acting half-back. All other players are out of play if they have not retired 10 m behind their own player who is taking part in the play-the-ball, in the case of the defending side, and 5 m in the case of the attacking side (i.e. the side in possession of the ball).

The referee is advised to act as a 'marker' for the side not in possession by standing on its side of the play-the-ball at a distance of, in his judgement, 10 m from it.

It is permissible for a tackled player to rise quickly to his feet and play the ball to himself if a player from the opposition has not taken up the position of marker standing immediately opposite the player who is playing the ball.

The scrum

A scrum (or 'scrummage') is formed to restart the game after the ball has gone into touch, after certain infringements, and when, in the opinion of the referee, it would be dangerous to the players to allow the game to proceed.

A scrum is formed when an injured player happens to be in possession and cannot resume playing. A scrum is also formed if the ball is loose at the time the game is stopped.

If a player is injured and continuance of play would be dangerous to him, and at that particular time a player in possession of the ball is tackled, the referee can stop the play and recommence it with the play-the-ball.

The laws state that no more than seven players may act as backs during the scrum. Thus no more than six players from each team may assist in the formation of a scrum.

The scrum is formed in most cases where the infringement occurred, but must never be formed less than 10 m from the touch line or 10 m from the goal line. When a scrum offence occurs, the penalty is awarded where the scrum should have been formed in the first place.

The referee must be on the alert to detect the first offender at a scrum and penalise him.

The pack

The normal pack consists of three forwards in the front row, two in the second, and a 'loose forward' who packs between the second row forwards with his shoulders pushing

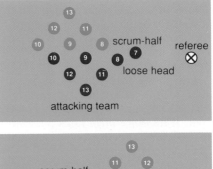

▲ *Fig. 13   Correct scrum formation*

against their buttocks. The second row packs in a similar position behind the front row.

The front row forwards of each team bind together with their arms, and interlock arms and heads with the opposing front row forwards in order to form a clear tunnel between the rows. The tunnel formed is at right angles to the touch line.

The front row forward who packs nearest to the referee has what is known as the 'loose head'. The non-offending side must always have the loose head, except in the case of a mutual infringement in which case the loose head is awarded to the attacking side.

The referee may stand on either side of the scrum.

Fig. 13 illustrates the correct formation for all scrums, and shows how the scrum forms with the loose head of the attacking team on the same side as the referee.

The scrum-half

The scrum-half of the non-offending side rolls the ball along the ground into the centre of the tunnel from the side on which the referee is standing. He must then immediately retire behind his own pack of forwards. The other players acting as backs must retire 5 m or more behind the last row of forwards of their respective teams in the scrum, and must remain so until the ball has emerged correctly from the scrum, otherwise a differential penalty may be awarded where the scrum was formed.

The hooker

When the ball hits the ground in the tunnel the two hookers may 'strike' for the ball, the object being to heel it to the scrum-half. The hooker may 'strike' for the ball with either foot. All other forwards must keep both feet on the ground.

The hooker should not have one arm loose during a scrum but should pack with both arms over the shoulders of the two supporting front row forwards. Players must not handle the ball in the scrum or intentionally fall or kneel down.

The ball must emerge from the scrum between and behind the second row of forwards, i.e. by the paths

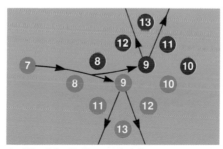

▲ *Fig. 14 Ball emerging from scrum*

shown in fig. 14, and when it does it is in play. The referee must penalise any player who deliberately commits an infringement or prevents the proper formation of a scrum.

Kicking

There are three types of kick employed in the game, as follows.

The punt

A player is said to punt the ball when he drops it from his hands and kicks it before it touches the ground.

A punt may be made in any direction and is useful for finding touch or gaining ground. The ball is kicked with the instep and an expert can impart a spiral motion to the ball which gives the kick extra length and accuracy.

A goal *cannot* be scored from a punt.

The drop kick

A player drop kicks the ball when he drops it from his hands to the ground and kicks it immediately it rebounds, i.e. a half-volley.

A drop kick is used:

● to recommence the game after dead ball from an unsuccessful penalty kick at goal and after certain other dead-ball situations (*see* page 12)
● to score a goal during play.

A drop goal counts one point.

The place kick

A place kick is made by a player placing the ball on the ground and then running forwards and kicking it.

It is used:

● to start the game and recommence it after the interval or after points have been scored

● to kick at goal after a try has been scored, in which case the kick is taken from any point opposite where the try was scored and parallel to the touch line
● to kick at goal after the award of a penalty kick, the kick being taken from the point on or behind where the penalty was awarded.

There are various ways of place kicking favoured by players, the two most popular being illustrated in figs 15 and 16.

A good kicker takes infinite care when placing the ball, and after sighting the goal does not take his eyes off the ball until after he has kicked it.

▲ *Fig. 15   Kicking with the toe of the boot*

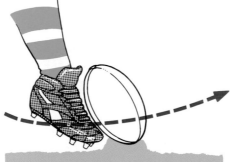

▲ *Fig. 16   Kicking with the instep*

The penalty kick

The referee awards a penalty kick to the non-offending team in the case of certain infringements which can be grouped under the following headings.

● Deliberate disobeyance of the laws.
● Foul play (*see* page 22).
● Obstruction (*see* pages 22–3).
● Offside play (*see* pages 23–7).
● Technical offences at the scrum.

The penalty kick may be a drop kick, a place kick or a punt, and is taken at any point on or behind the spot where the infringement occurred and the same distance from the touch line. The object of the kick may be: (a) to score a goal from a drop kick or place kick; (b) to gain ground by kicking for touch, in which case the kicker's side is allowed to place the ball on the ground 10 m in from the point of entry into touch, and recommence play with another kick (a goal cannot be scored from this second kick; usually the player taking it tap kicks and regains possession); or (c) to recommence play without delay by kicking the ball in any direction from the mark, the ball remaining in the field of play (again the player usually tap kicks and regains possession).

When the penalty kick is taken, the following rules must be observed.

● All players of the kicker's side must be behind the ball when it is kicked. When a player intends to kick at goal from a penalty award and moves back from the mark in order to improve his angle, then the mark automatically moves back to where he places the ball and opponents can then advance to within 10 m of this new mark.
● Players of the offending side must retire 10 m, towards their own goal line, from the mark.
● Players of the offending side must not charge the kick, or raise their hands above their heads.

For an infringement by the kicker's team the referee awards a scrum at the point where the kick was awarded.

For an infringement by the offending team the kick is either retaken or another penalty is awarded where the

offence took place – whichever is to the advantage of the non-offending side.

If a player signifies that he intends to kick at goal from a penalty award, then he must make a genuine attempt and not deceive the opposition by commencing play with a tap kick. However, he is not obliged to kick it 10 m or even to pass the mark; he can take a tap kick in the first place.

For technical offences at the scrum (for example, foot up, loose arm, illegal binding, improper feeding or offside by any player), the differential penalty operates. The non-offending side may either kick for touch or take a tap kick. They may not, however, kick at goal from a differential penalty awarded to them.

Referee's signals

When the game is stopped it is the duty of the referee to signal his decision and, where necessary, the nature of the infringement. After the referee has blown his whistle he indicates his decision as to how the game shall be recommenced by making the appro-

priate approved signal. He then indicates the nature of the infringement.

These signals are of great benefit both to the player and the spectator; it is not uncommon to hear the spectator shout: 'What's that for?' when the referee awards a penalty against his side. If he knew the signals he could tell without any trouble whether it was for a loose arm in the scrum or the scrum-half feeding his own feet, for example. It is quite impossible to tell from the touch line what infringements have occurred in a scrum unless the referee issues a signal and a knowledgeable player or spectator understands the signal.

Some common signals are shown in figs 17–22. The first one is for a penalty kick: the referee faces the non-offending team and extends his right arm as shown. The second indicates obstruction. Fig. 19 shows that the prop has illegally raised his foot and has tried to strike for the ball; the referee raises his foot and points to the offending player. Fig. 20 indicates dissent. Fig. 21 indicates that the scrum-half has fed his own feet. Fig. 22 shows that a forward pass has occurred.

▲ Fig. 17
Penalty kick

▲ Fig. 18
Obstruction

▲ Fig. 19 Prop has illegally raised his foot and tried to strike for the ball

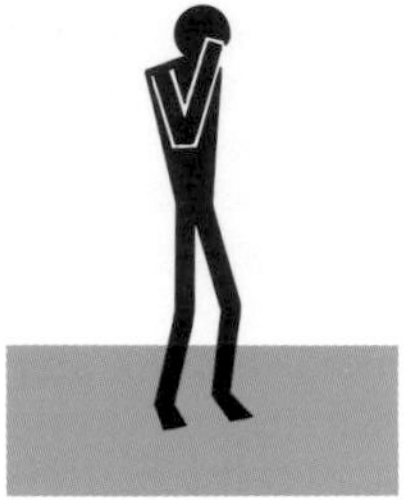

▲ Fig. 20
Dissent
(blows whistle)

▲ Fig. 21
Scrum-half has fed his own feet

▲ Fig. 22
Forward pass

Foul play

A penalty is awarded against a player committing foul play.

Tripping

A player is not allowed to trip an opponent with his foot. The referee may order the offender from the field of play.

Striking

A player is not allowed to strike, or attempt to strike, an opponent with his fist or any part of his arm. The referee may order the offender from the field of play.

Note Handing off is allowed as mentioned in 'Tackling' (*see* pages 16–17).

Kicking

A player is not allowed to kick at an opponent or recklessly kick at the ball when an opponent is picking it up, or when it may cause injury to an opponent. The referee may order the offender from the field of play.

Obstruction

A player is obstructing an opponent if he deliberately:

● impedes his progress when running towards the ball
● tackles him after he has kicked the ball, thus preventing him from following up the kick
● tackles or impedes any player who is not in possession of the ball.

For these offences a penalty is awarded.
It should be noted that when two opposing players are running side by

side towards a ball, a shoulder charge is permitted, but not the use of hands or arms. In the second example it is often difficult for a player to halt a tackle made just as the opponent is about to kick, and it is left to the referee's discretion whether the tackle was made deliberately after the kick or not.

If a penalty is given it is awarded where the ball bounces (if kicked forwards), or 10 m from the touch line opposite to where it leaves the field of play if it is kicked out on the full.

If a penalty is given it is awarded where the ball bounces (if kicked forwards) or 10 m from the touch line opposite to where it leaves the field of play if it is kicked out on the full.

If offences warranting penalties occur in touch then the offenders can still be penalised and the mark is made 10 m infield from the touch line opposite where the offence occurred. In the case priate line, i.e. the centre of the half-way line, the centre of the 20-metre line or the centre of the 10-metre from goal line, as the case may be. If a defending side offends in its own in-goal and the offence would normally warrant a penalty award, the mark is

made 10 m from the goal line in the field of play opposite where the offence was committed.

Offside

A player is in an offside position anywhere between his own goal line and the opponents' dead-ball line when he is in front of a player of his own side who is in possession of the ball, or who last touched the ball. In fig. 23, A and B are offside.

Any player who is not nearer to his own goal line than the tackled player shall be offside and shall be penalised if he gains or attempts to gain an unfair

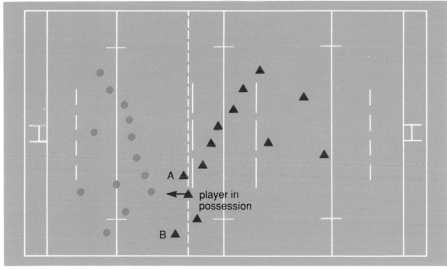

player in
possession

▲ Fig. 23   A and B are offside

advantage, provided that such penalty is not to the disadvantage of the non-offending side.

An offside player must not take any part in the game or attempt in any way to influence the course of the game. He must not encroach within 10 m of an opponent who is waiting for the ball, and must immediately retire 10 m from any opponent who first secures possession.

If a player in an offside position plays or attempts to play the ball, or tackles or attempts to tackle an opponent, the referee may award a penalty kick to the opponents at the place where the infringement occurred. The referee will, of course, allow play to proceed if the non-offending side have an advantage.

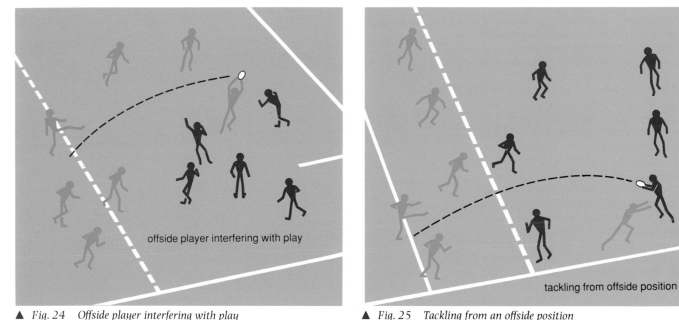

offside player interfering with play

tackling from offside position

▲ *Fig. 24   Offside player interfering with play*

▲ *Fig. 25   Tackling from an offside position*

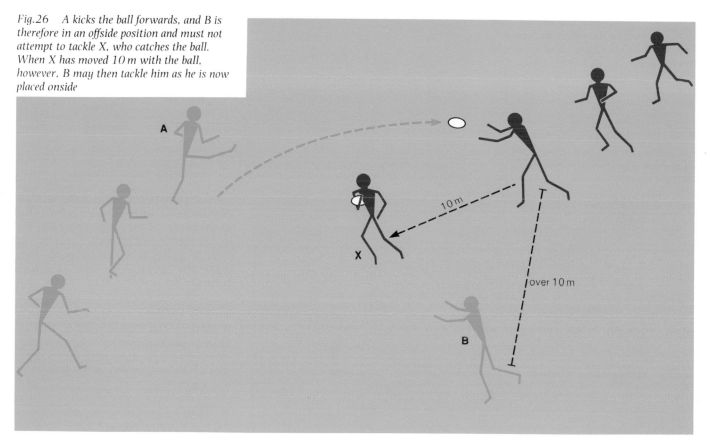

Fig.26   A kicks the ball forwards, and B is therefore in an offside position and must not attempt to tackle X, who catches the ball. When X has moved 10 m with the ball, however, B may then tackle him as he is now placed onside

10 m

over 10 m

A

X

B

▶ *Fig. 27   B is in an offside position when A kicks the ball and it is caught by X. When X passes the ball to Y, B is placed onside and may tackle Y*

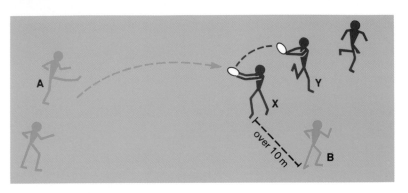

▼ *Fig. 28   When A receives the ball, B and C are offside; but as A runs forwards with the ball in his possession he passes B and C, placing them onside*

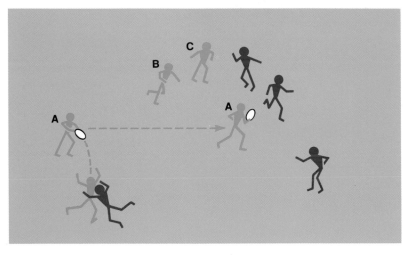

When offside play occurs at a kick-off or a drop-out, a penalty kick is awarded at the centre of the appropriate line or, in the case of a drop-out from between the posts, the penalty is awarded 10 m from the goal line and mid-way between the posts.

Placed onside

A player in an offside position can be placed onside, provided he is not within 10 m of an opponent who has possession of the ball, by any of the following movements:

● when an opponent in possession of the ball has run 10 m

- when the ball has been kicked or passed by an opponent
- when a player of his own side in possession of the ball has run in front of him
- when the player of his own side in possession of the ball kicks the ball when behind him and then runs in front of him. Only the kicker can put the player onside.

Examples of placed onside are shown in figs 26–9.

In all of these cases B and C must be 10 m or more from an opponent who gets possession of the ball. If the kicker follows up by running into touch, he must return to the field of play before he can put other players onside.

▲ *Fig. 29   A kicks the ball forwards and B, standing onside, follows up quickly. B cannot place C onside by running past him – only the kicker can do this. Once B has touched the ball, however, all his own players behind him will be onside*

Basic skills

Running with the ball

Rugby league is essentially a running game in which retaining possession of the ball is vital. A player running with the ball should hold it firmly in both hands in preparation for a swift pass to a supporting team-mate. If, however, a player is attempting to beat an opponent's tackle, usually the ball will be held close to the lower chest, using one hand and the forearm. At all times the first inclination of a player in possession of the ball should be to run straight and with great determination. Good players are distinguished by their ability to 'read the game', i.e. at all times to be aware of the dispositions both of their own supporting players and of the opposing defenders.

Passing the ball

Swift, accurate passing of the ball is the key to breaching the opposition's defence and setting up scoring positions.

The ball should be held with fingers outspread underneath, palms facing inwards. The thumbs should be placed on the upper part of the ball, holding it in position. The arms should be held relaxed, with elbows slightly bent and close to the side, so that the ball can be swung in either direction, left or right.

The target area is in front of the intended receiver between the lower chest and waist (often referred to as the 'bread basket').

To transfer the ball accurately, the upper part of the body should be twisted at the hips, bringing the shoulders square to the intended receiver. The arms swing the ball well back, and then move across the body, releasing the ball towards the target area with a flat trajectory. The ball should not be lobbed. The path of the ball, therefore, is directed by the fingers and wrists, with the arms following through so that they are fully extended in the direction of the intended receiver, fingers pointing at the target area.

Obviously, all players must be able to take a pass as well as execute one. As with many facets of the game, absolute concentration is the key note here, because in the heat of play the receiver often has to hold a pass, the direction of which is behind the target area or higher or lower than the ideal. To receive a pass, the trunk should be turned to face the passer with the eyes remaining fixed on the ball as it leaves the passer's hands. The arms and fingers should be extended towards the ball in its flight. Whenever possible, both hands should be used to receive the ball and draw it into the body to secure possession. The receiver should not reduce pace in order to take the pass.

As well as the ability to pass on the run, proficiency at passing the ball direct from the ground is vital, since this kind of pass is used in most play-the-ball and scrummage situations. Therefore, a pass from the ground is the first act of most attacking play. It is essential that the passer is fully aware of the position of the first receiver, and accurately assesses how much pace and strength the pass should carry. The body should be bent over the ball, which is held firmly in both hands. Speed is essential, so that the pass is made without lifting the ball from the

▲ *Passing: fully extended follow-through*

ground or straightening the back. The feet should straddle the ball at a comfortable distance, with the 'outside' foot pointing in the direction of the receiver. The target area is the same as for the pass on the move and the ball is directed by the fingers and wrists with a clear follow-through by the arms towards the receiver.

Evasion

Rugby league is an exciting spectator sport. Much of its appeal derives from the individual skills used by players to beat the intended tackles of their immediate opposition, thus finding space for exciting running and free-flowing passing which can bring a crowd to its feet. The most widely used methods of evasion are outlined below.

The side-step

The side-step involves a sudden change of direction to beat an opponent who is already committed to making a tackle. To side-step to the left, as the would-be tackler is approached, the toes of the

Swerve ▶

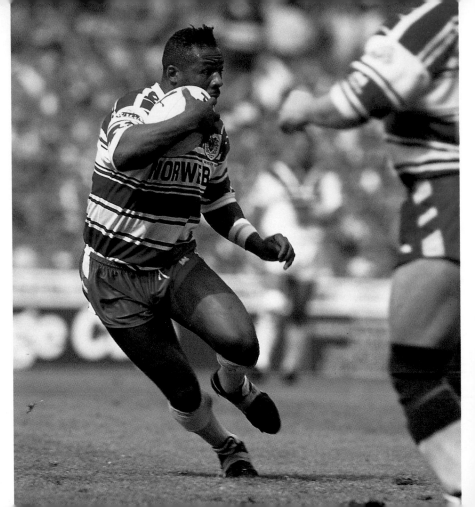

right foot are driven hard into the ground, and the runner thrusts himself across, transferring his weight to the left foot which is driven hard into the ground on contact, enabling the runner to continue on a straight line in a new direction, leaving the defender in his wake. The runner should not shorten his stride as he approaches the defender, and the head should remain still throughout the movement, which should be executed at maximum speed. Good players should be able to side-step in both directions. For the side-step to the right, the opposite actions apply.

The swerve

The swerve involves the runner changing direction on a route which takes him round the would-be tackler in a movement left late but not as extreme as the side step. Good footwork and exact timing are vital. To swerve to the right, the runner balances on the outside of his right foot, and the inside of his left foot, running in an arc away from the defender with the hips also swaying away from the would-be tackler. In swerving to the left, the balance points are reversed.

▲ *The hand-off* (see *page 32*)

31

The hand-off

To execute an effective hand-off, the runner transfers the ball to one hand; with a strong thrust of the arm he uses the other hand, open palm outwards, to push or fend off the would-be tackler with a forceful stabbing motion into his chest, head or shoulder. When contact is made, the arm should be straightened immediately. Accurate timing is essential to enable the runner either to push the tackler away and down, or to use the defender's own momentum to propel himself away from the tackle. The hand-off is often combined with the side-step or swerve.

The bump-off

This is a method of breaking a tackle in which the ball-carrier uses a hard part of the body, particularly the shoulder or the hip, to knock or bump off the would-be tackler. The ball-carrier must run with great determination, and at the moment of contact the legs must be driven hard into the ground in order to generate the necessary momentum which will carry the runner through the intended tackle. The chest may also be used to bump off a defender. In this technique, the ball-carrier should fold his arms over the ball, elbows downwards, with the brunt of the impact being taken on his forearms.

Hit and spin

On the point of contact, the ball-carrier dips his shoulder and spins off and away from the defender, at which point he can continue to make ground himself or pass the ball to a supporting team-mate. The runner should take short steps as the collision point is approached, and the legs should pump vigorously throughout the action.

Change of pace

The ball-carrier always holds a potential advantage over the defenders in that he should know what he intends to do next in order to beat the would-be tackler. Deception, causing uncertainty in the mind of the defender, is one of the most potent weapons in the attacking player's armoury. Change of pace is one of the most effective techniques in which deception is used to the ball-carrier's advantage.

Change of pace involves a sudden acceleration which causes the defender to mistime his tackle. As he approaches the would-be tackler, the runner slows down a little causing the defender to alter his positioning and adjust his timing for the tackle. The ball-carrier then moves suddenly into top gear, lengthening his stride and accelerating quickly away from the tackle.

The dummy

To execute a dummy pass, the ball-carrier acts in every respect as if he is about to make a pass, following through with the arms in the direction of the intended receiver. At the last moment the ball-carrier draws the ball back, retaining possession. The aim is to persuade the defenders to transfer their concentration away from the ball-carrier and towards his supporting players, one of whom they believe is about to receive his pass. To achieve this, it is essential that the dummy is absolutely convincing. The defenders (and, indeed, the spectators) must, for a crucial instant, really believe that the pass has been given.

▲ *A play-the-ball (see page 34)*

Play-the-ball

The play-the-ball is a unique and totally distinctive feature of rugby league football. The action is used to restart play immediately following a tackle. Some 300 or more play-the-balls take place in every game, and for the team in possession to sustain continuous attacks it is vital that each play-the-ball in a 'set of six' is quickly and smoothly executed. It is essential, therefore, that every player should master this fundamental skill.

In order to play the ball, the tackled player must first regain his feet as quickly as possible. Then, facing the opposition goal line, he should lift the ball clear of the ground. Bending his body well over the ball, he should then place it lengthways on the ground in front of and alongside his leading foot. Simultaneously, the sole of the other foot is placed on top of the ball and the ball is rolled back under complete control.

The player immediately behind the one playing the ball, the acting half-back, must transfer the ball swiftly to the first receiver, passing the ball

▲ *A solid tackle*

34

directly from the ground, unless he elects to run himself.

It should be noted that, since the play-the-ball is effectively a two-man scrummage, once the player playing the ball has placed it on the ground the defender marking him is permitted to strike for the ball in an attempt to hook it back, thus gaining possession for his side. At the play-the-ball, the ball may be played with the foot in any direction, though in the vast majority of situations it will be rolled back to the acting half-back's hands. If the defence is caught napping by a particularly quick play-the-ball, and do not provide a marker, the player playing the ball may play it to himself by tapping it forwards into his own hands and thus continuing the attack.

Tackling

Although rugby league is essentially a running and handling game, strong, well-organised and totally committed defence is the foundation of winning rugby. Effective tackling requires accurate timing, good technique, determination and, since a smaller player is often called on to knock down a much larger player running at pace, no little courage. However, once a player has mastered the various techniques, great pleasure and satisfaction can be gained by achieving a high tackle count.

There are four basic tackles which all players must strive to master. These are:

● tackles from the side, the rear, and the front, all of which aim to knock the ball-carrier to the ground
● the smother tackle, where the aim is to pinion the ball-carrier's arms so that he cannot pass to a supporting team-mate.

Certain important elements are common requirements for tackles made from the side or from the rear. These are as follows.

● The target area is the opponent's thigh.
● The shoulder should be driven powerfully into the opponent's thigh.
● The arms should encircle the opponent's thighs, the hands linking and gripping hard.

● The grip must be maintained until the opponent is fully grounded.
● The tackler should always try to finish on top as the tackle is completed.

The position of the tackler's head is most important in effecting a successful tackle and ensuring that the tackler himself is not hurt in the process.

For the orthodox tackle from the side, the head must always be placed behind the opponent.

For the tackle from the rear, the head should be placed at the side of the opponent, and as the hands link to secure a firm hold they should be slid down the ball-carrier's legs.

Because many of the physical confrontations in rugby league are head-to-head, it is absolutely essential that all players learn to tackle from a front-on position. To successfully tackle an opponent head-on and moving at pace, it is not so much a question of the tackler's size as his courage, determination and sense of timing.

There are two types of head-on tackle: a more passive version, in which the ball-carrier's own weight and momentum are used against him;

and a more aggressive variety in which the ball-carrier is lifted and forced backwards in a powerful drive by the tackler (often referred to as the 'block-buster').

The following points should be applied when making the basic 'passive' tackle from in front.

● The target area is the opponent's thigh.
● The tackler's head should be placed. at the side of the ball-carrier.
● The tackler blocks the thighs of the opponent with his shoulder.
● The tackler's arms encircle the ball-carrier's legs. Hands link and grip tight.
● The opponent's own weight and momentum are used to make the tackle effective
● The ball-carrier should be rolled on to his side.
● The tackler should endeavour to finish on top as the tackle is completed.

To effect a blockbuster tackle the tackler must move quickly into position and, if possible, before the ball-carrier has had time to build up maxi-

mum pace. The following basic principles apply.

● The target area is the opponent's waist.
● The tackler should move quickly forwards into an effective tackling position
● The tackler's shoulder should be driven powerfully into the opponent's waist.
● The head of the tackler should be placed at the side of the ball-carrier.
● The tackler's arms encircle the opponent's body below his centre of gravity, i.e. below the buttocks.
● The arms encircle the opponent, hands link and grip tight.
● The tackler then drives powerfully with his legs, pulling and lifting his opponent using the arms and shoulder.
● The opponent is driven backwards and on to the ground.
● The tackler should finish on top of his opponent, with his shoulder still buried into the target area.

It is most important that an opponent, even when tackled, should not be allowed to off-load the ball to a support-

ing team-mate. Therefore, the second player into the tackle must have the ability to smother the ball. The smother tackle can also be effectively employed when the tackler is isolated, facing a ball-carrying opponent who has support. A determined tackle, clamping the ball-carrier's arms, will often succeed in preventing the ball being transferred to a supporting colleague.

For the smother tackle to be effective, the following principles must be applied.

● Though the basic target is the ball, the eyes should never leave the ball-carrier, for to do so invites accepting a dummy pass.
● The tackler must move quickly forwards into a tackling position.
● The arms should be wrapped powerfully around the upper part of the opponent's body.
● The ball should be pinned between the tackler's body and that of his opponent.
● The arms of the ball-carrier must be pinioned to his sides.
● Whenever possible, the opponent should be forced to the ground.

The most effective smother tackle is likely to be made when the tackler approaches his opponent from the outside.

Kicking

Though rugby league is essentially a game based on running, passing and tackling, kicking, especially as a tactical ploy, is also an important and – when well executed – a welcome element. In addition, points gained by a successful place kick (a conversion following the scoring of a try, or a penalty kick at goal), or from a dropped goal in broken play, can make all the difference between victory and defeat.

Most teams designate specialist kickers, whether it be for tactical kicks aimed at gaining ground, for placing the opposition under extreme pressure, or for place kicks and dropped goal efforts. However, it is most useful for all players to master the basic skills of the kicking game.

The basic techniques involved in executing the five most frequently used types of kick now follow.

The punt

The punt is a variety of kick in which the ball is released from the hands and kicked before it touches the ground. It is used to gain ground from a penalty kick by kicking the ball directly out of play and into touch, or to gain ground directly from play, in which case the ball must first bounce inside the field of play before crossing the touch line.

As an attacking ploy, the punt is often used in the form of a very high kick, placed deep behind the opposition's defensive line, or, more usually, aimed at the opposition's full back. It is essential that team-mates of the kicker follow up fast in order either to regain possession or contain the opposition deep in their own territory should they secure the ball.

For a well-executed punt, the following techniques must be applied.

● The ball should be held as if making a pass.
● The shoulders should be squared and pointed at the target.
● Keep the head down and the eyes glued on the ball until the kick has been made.
● The ball should be held a comfortable distance away from the body.
● The hands guide the ball down to the point where contact is made with the foot.
● The rounded part of the ball is contacted by the top of the foot.
● The ankle should be flexed on contact, thus straightening the toes.
● The foot drives through the ball after contact with a full follow-through of the kicking leg towards the target.

A common variation of the orthodox punt described above is the 'torpedo'. This technique is used when the kicker's aim is to gain as much ground as possible with his kick.

When preparing to execute a torpedo punt, a right-handed kicker should place his right hand slightly under and to the rear right side of the ball, with his left hand in a similar position underneath and to the front left side. The ball should be pointed slightly inwards and the kicking foot should be angled slightly inwards also as it makes contact with the ball. Correct execution of the torpedo punt imparts a spinning, 'rifling' effect on the flight of the ball which enables the kicker to gain valuable extra distance.

The grubber

This kick is a useful variant, often employed to break a strong tackling defence, against which powerful running and passing movements have had little effect.

The aim is for the ball to be 'slotted' between two opposing players as they move up in a defensive line. The short kick takes the ball into space behind the opponents' defensive line and ideally makes the ball roll point-over-point, eventually bouncing up to allow a team-mate following through from an onside position to regain possession and so continue the attack.

In executing the grubber kick, the ball is held as for making a pass, but slightly lower than for the punt. The foot should make contact with the top of the ball just before the ball strikes the ground, with the kicking knee bent and the head well over the ball. The kicking foot should be flexed from the ankle as the foot drives the ball into the ground, thus imparting the desired rolling motion to the ball. The foot should

▲ *Preparing to take a place kick*

make contact with the ball in a stabbing motion with no follow-through.

The kick-over or chip kick

As with the grubber, this technique is used in order to breach a well-organised defence. In this case, however, the ball is kicked over the heads of the defenders, again with the aim of enabling a team-mate to follow up and re-gather the ball.

Basic techniques are the same as for the punt, except that the kicking foot is slightly flexed and should *not* follow through. The ball should travel only a short distance, so correct 'weighting' of the kick is vital. It is also important that the kicker should be able to execute this particular kick while travelling at speed.

The place kick

The place kick is used to start and restart a game, or to kick for goal.

The traditional method of executing a place kick was for the kicker to approach the ball from a front-on position and strike the ball with his toe-end. These days, however, by far the most common technique is the round-the-corner method, in which the kicker approaches the ball in a curved run-up and strikes it with the instep, as if kicking a soccer ball.

Each of these methods has its own particular strengths and weaknesses.

The strength of the toe-end method is that the kicker, the ball and the target are in a straight line. Thus good technique ensures accuracy. However, since the correct spot where the foot should make contact with the ball is very small, this technique affords little margin for error.

The round-the-corner method enables the kicker to gain greater distance because more leverage from the hip and thigh is obtained. However, since the ensuing trajectory of the ball is often curved, accuracy is not always assured, especially when a right-footed kicker is kicking from the right-hand side of the field.

The toe-end kick

The laws of the game permit the kicker to raise the ball from the ground by means of a tee. Traditionally the tee comprises a small mound of soil and grass dug by use of the heel and/or the toe. However, these days many kickers prefer to use a small mound of sand on which to 'sit' the ball, and the use of specially made plastic tees, long used in American football, is becoming increasingly common.

● The ball should be made to sit on the tee in such a way that a central point approximately 25 mm from the bottom of the ball is clearly in sight. This becomes the target area and is often referred to as the 'spot'. It is a useful aid to accuracy to aim a seam of the ball at the target.

● Kicker, ball and target should be in a straight line.

● Standing directly behind the ball, the kicker should then place the non-kicking foot alongside and close to the ball, while the kicking foot is placed directly behind it.

● The body should be bent directly over the ball, and a final eye check made to ensure that the seam is aimed at the target and that kicker, ball and target are still directly in line.

● With head bent, the eyes should gaze at the spot, the target area, and must remain glued to the target area until the ball is kicked.

● Maintaining absolute concentration, the kicker should then retire the required number of backward steps (this will depend on individual preference).

● With total composure the kicker should then move slowly forwards towards the ball with a balanced, rhythmic motion.

● The non-kicking foot is placed directly next to the ball with the body well over the ball, head bent.

● The toe must make contact with the spot, the foot and kicking leg following through powerfully directly towards the target.

● The shoulders should be square and level, arms outstretched as necessary to ensure perfect balance.

The round-the-corner method

The basic techniques are the same, except that:

● the kicker's approach to the ball should describe a curved arc with just the final two, vital strides being straight on

● the ball should be struck with the instep or inside of the foot

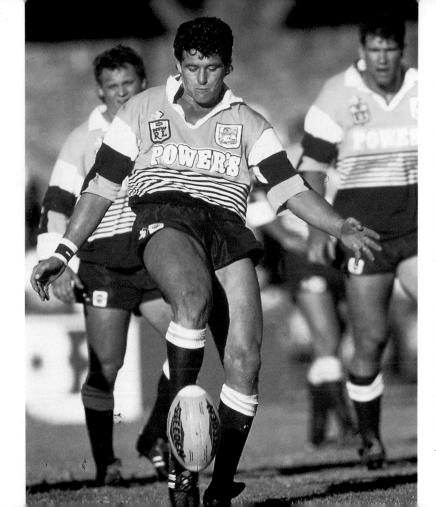

● the non-kicking foot is placed slightly further away from the ball, thus imparting a more powerful swing of the hip and thigh.

The drop kick

The drop kick is used to restart the game from a dead-ball situation, or to score one point by kicking the ball over the bar from broken play.

The basic techniques are very similar to those adopted for the orthodox punt, except that the foot makes contact with the ball just as it touches the ground. The kicker should glance briefly in the direction of the target area, after which his eyes should concentrate on the kicking area where the foot will make contact with the ball. The ball is held away from the body as for a pass, and then adjusted to an angle approximately 45° relative to the ground. The ball should be guided to the ground at this same angle so that it will strike the ground beside the toes of the non-kicking foot. The ball should be struck with the lower part of the instep. not with the toes, and the head

◀ *Executing a drop kick*